10 Patterns for Carving Whales

Brian Gilmore

D1609687

Schiffer Publishing Ltd

77 Lower Valley Road, Atglen, PA 19310

Dedication

To Anne, my wonderful wife and helper, and our great family who have helped me to arrive safely and happily to this plateau in my life.

Printed in China

ISBN: 0-88740-855-9

Book Design by Audrey L. Whiteside.

Library of Congress Cataloging-in-Publication Data

Gilmore, Brian, 1935-
    10 patterns for carving whales/Brian Gilmore.
      p. cm.--(A schiffer book for woodcarvers)
    ISBN 0-88740-855-9
    1. Wood-carving--Patterns. 2. Whales in art.
I. Title. II. Series.
TT199.7.G55 1995
731'.832--dc20   95-22367
                        CIP

Published by Schiffer Publishing, Ltd.
77 Lower Valley Road
Atglen, PA 19310
Please write for a free catalog.
This book may be purchased from the publisher.
Please include $2.95 postage.
Try your bookstore first.

We are interested in hearing from authors
with book ideas on related subjects.

Contents

Foreword

A few years ago, I was asked by a client for a whale carving. When I asked what kind of whale, they replied, "Oh you know, one of those big ones like Moby Dick."

This book has grown out of that simple request, and a more fascinating and diverse subject matter would be hard to find.

All of the projects in this book can be made as simple or as complex as the carver desires.

I hope you will find as much enjoyment as I have in carving these mysterious creatures.

Brian Gilmore, Hamilton 1994.

Introduction

There are seventy-six species of whales swimming around in our oceans. With this book you should be able to carve most of them. A few minor adaptations and color changes is all that will be needed.

There is a lot of mystery surrounding whales. Where do they come from? How have they evolved? It is believed that whales came out of the oceans, adapted to earth's environment, and then returned to the oceans, and have readapted again to that underwater world. In some whales, a vestige of a pelvis and lower limbs can still be found. Beneath their flippers is a bone structure incredibly similar to the human arm and hand.

Why do whales sing? How do they sing? They have no vocal cords. Scientists have recorded the wonderfully eerie haunting songs of the humpback whale and feel they are love songs, but why does only the humpback sing.

Why do whales strand themselves on beaches around the world and then refuse to be helped? This phenomenon has occurred for years, and is the subject of ongoing investigations by scientists.

What do we know? We know, that they are not fish, but warm blooded, air breathing mammals that copulate, give birth, wean their young, and have some form of family or social structure.

Man has hunted and slaughtered whales for their blubber, their oil, baleen and meat for 4,000 years. Whale bones have been discovered in prehistoric digs. Drawings of harpooned whales have been found on cave walls. Had we not stopped hunting when we did, most of the whales in this book would be extinct, not endangered.

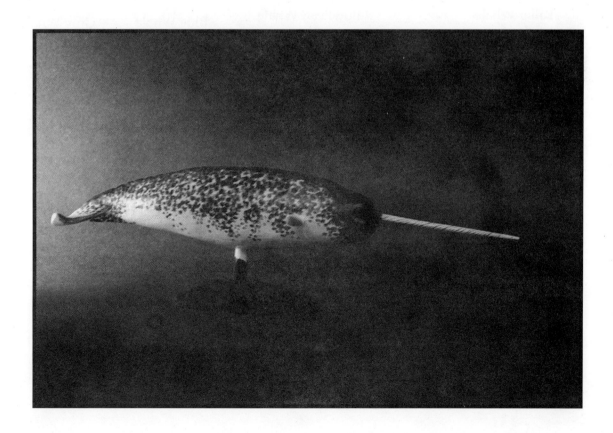

WHALE FAMILIES

There are two whale families in existence today. One family is Odontoceti, whales with teeth. The other is Mysticeti, whales that have baleen. Rorquals are whales that have pleated throats that expand for feeding. Some whales can hold 50 tons of water, shrimp, plankton or whatever in their throats.

The following chart is appropriate for this book only.

Whale Families

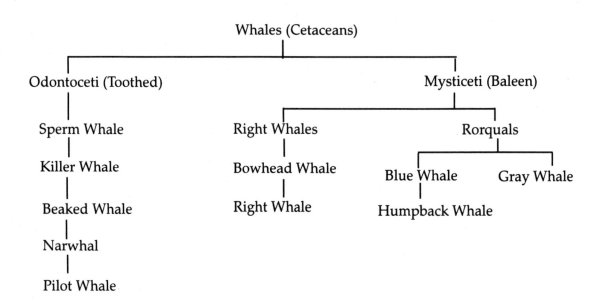

COMPARITIVE SIZES

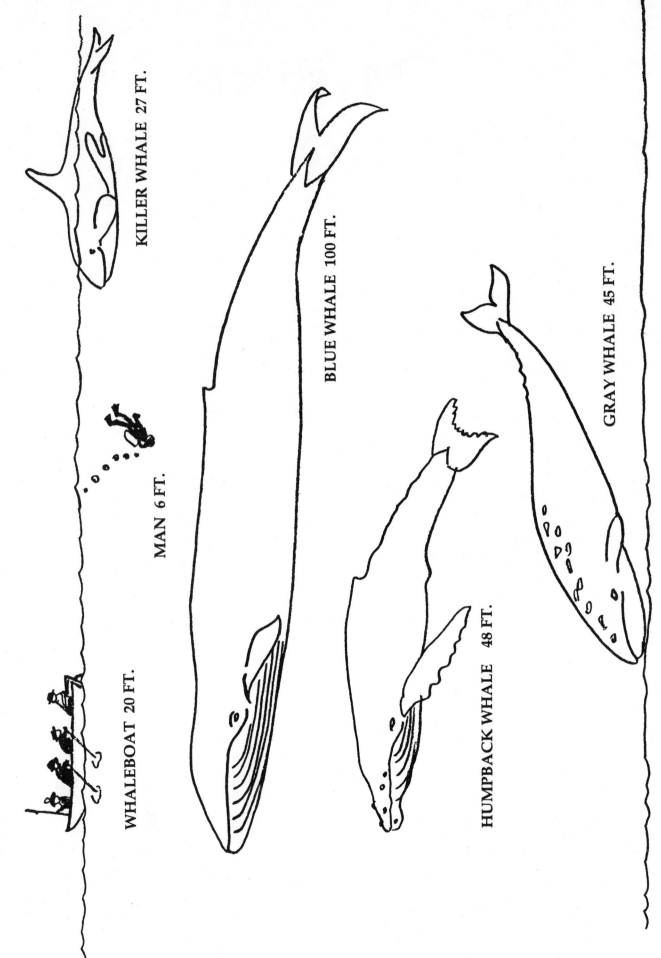

KILLER WHALE 27 FT.

BLUE WHALE 100 FT.

GRAY WHALE 45 FT.

MAN 6 FT.

WHALEBOAT 20 FT.

HUMPBACK WHALE 48 FT.

7

Mysticeti

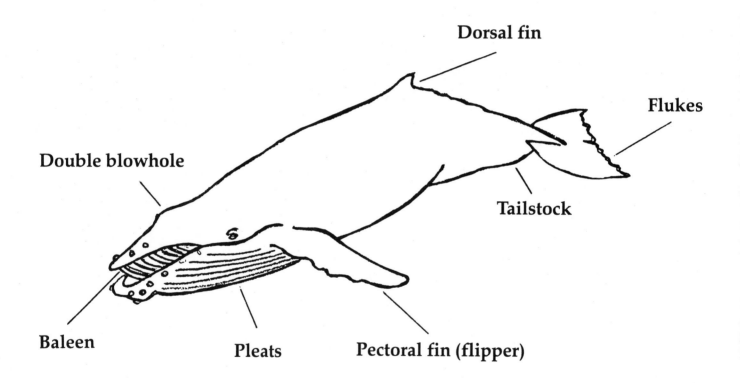

Dorsal fin

Flukes

Double blowhole

Tailstock

Baleen

Pleats

Pectoral fin (flipper)

Odonticeti

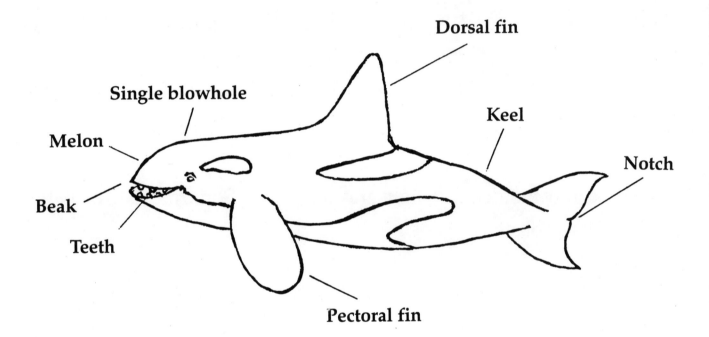

Single blowhole

Melon

Beak

Teeth

Dorsal fin

Keel

Notch

Pectoral fin

Blue Whale

LOCATION

World wide. All the oceans to the edge of polar seas. Moves to temperate waters to mate and give birth.

SIZE

Male	100 feet.	150 tons. Max. 196 tons.
Female	85 feet.	150 tons.
Calf	23 feet.	8 tons.

COLOR

Blue gray mottled with light gray and white. Some mustard on belly. Baleen is black.

FACTS

Largest animal ever to live on this planet. In 1931 over 30,000 blue whales were slaughtered and the species have never fully recovered.

STATUS

Endangered.

Blue Whale

Wood size: 3" x 3" x 11"

100 ft. 120 tons

Flukes are 20 ft. wide

Bony ridge on nose

There are approximately 75 pleats on throat

Dorsal fin approximately 1 ft.

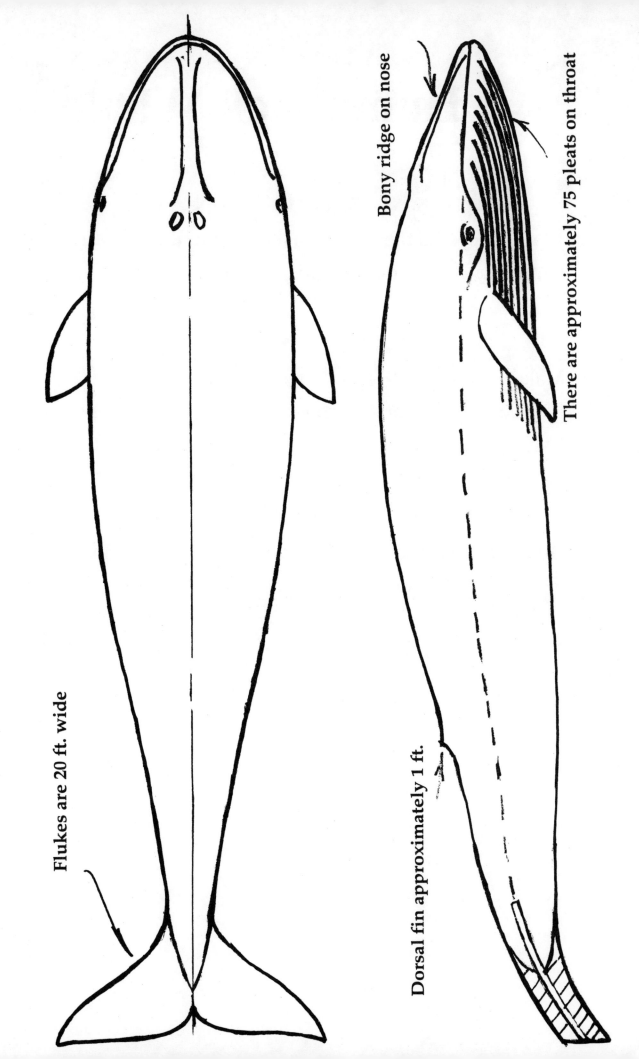

Humpback Whale

LOCATION

World wide. All the oceans to the edge of the polar seas. Moves to temperate waters to mate and give birth.

SIZE

Male	48 feet to max. 58 feet	45 tons.
Female	50 feet to max. 62 feet	45 tons.
Calf		1.5 tons.

COLOR

Blackish blue, white on throat pleats and under flippers. Flukes are mottled white underneath.

FACTS

Humpbacks have been protected since 1966. World population approximately 10,000.

STATUS

Endangered.

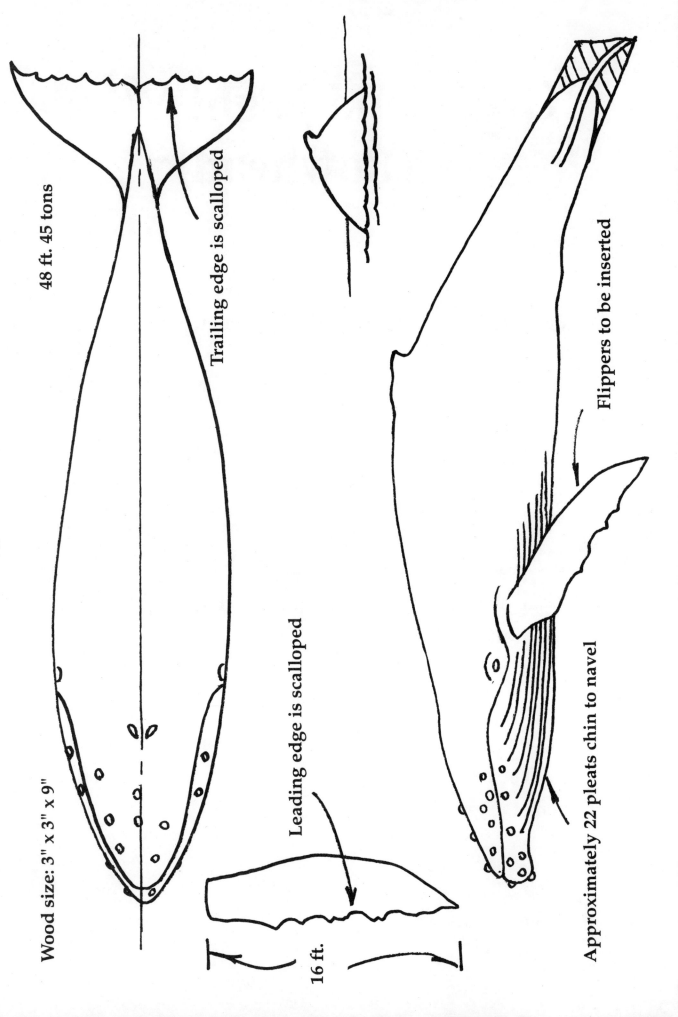

Humpback Whale

48 ft. 45 tons

Wood size: 3" x 3" x 9"

Trailing edge is scalloped

Leading edge is scalloped

16 ft.

Flippers to be inserted

Approximately 22 pleats chin to navel

Greenland Right Whale (Bowhead)

LOCATION

Found only in Arctic Ocean, Bering Strait to Greenland.

SIZE

Male	50 feet to max. 65 feet	110 tons.
Female	50 feet to max. 65 feet	110 tons.
Calf	12 feet	

COLOR

Black all over, except for white chin. Baleen dark gray or black with green metallic sheen.

FACTS

These whales were considered the "right" ones to catch, hence their name. They were slow and they had a large amount of blubber and baleen.

STATUS

Endangered.

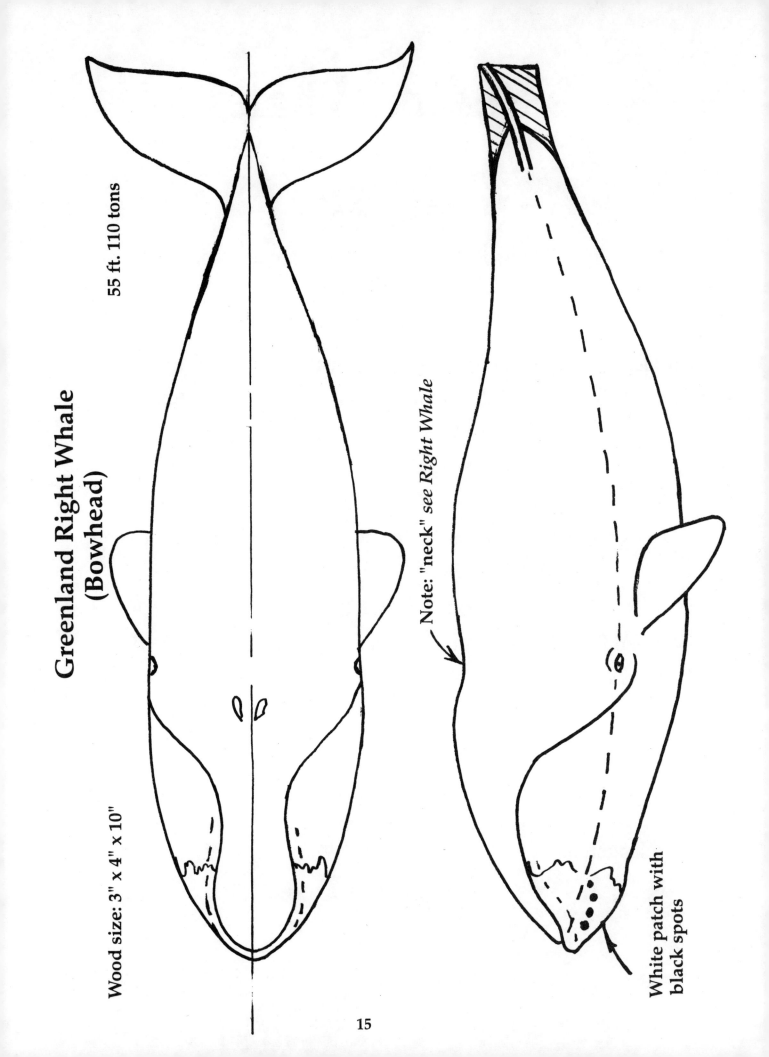

Greenland Right Whale
(Bowhead)

55 ft. 110 tons

Wood size: 3" x 4" x 10"

Note: "neck" *see Right Whale*

White patch with
black spots

Sperm Whale

LOCATION

World wide. All the oceans. Migrates toward equator in fall.

SIZE

Male	50 feet to max. 65 feet	40 tons.
Female	36 feet to max. 56 feet	22 tons.
Calf	15 feet	

COLOR

Dark gray, paler on belly. White under mouth and around upper lip.

FACTS

Valued for their sperm oil, found in their heads and for the Ambergris (used in perfume making). This whale has been detected on sonar at 10,000 feet below the surface. It has a brain six times the size of a human.

STATUS

Endangered.

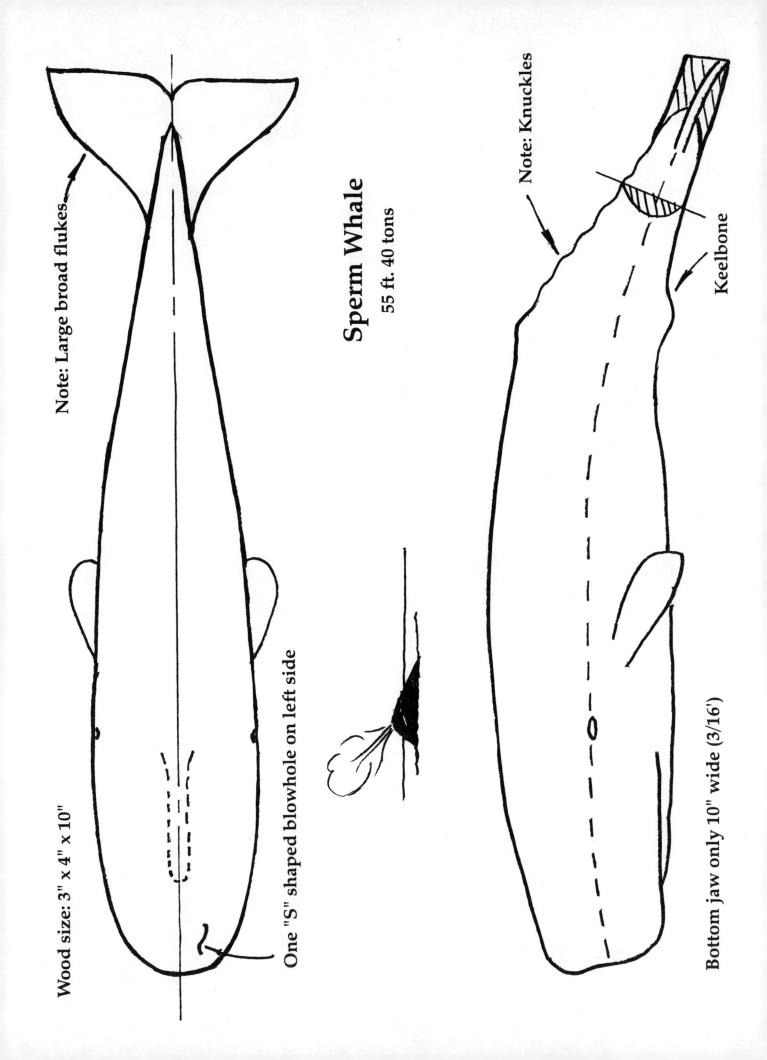

Note: Large broad flukes

Wood size: 3" x 4" x 10"

One "S" shaped blowhole on left side

Sperm Whale
55 ft. 40 tons

Note: Knuckles

Keelbone

Bottom jaw only 10" wide (3/16')

Great Right Whale

LOCATION

North Pacific, North Atlantic, Southern Oceans.

SIZE

Male	50 feet to max. 60 feet	60 tons.
Female	50 feet to max. 60 feet	60 tons.
Calf	17 feet	

Color

Black on top, white spots on chin and white around navel, horny growths are white/pink. Baleen dark olive gray.

FACTS

This again is a "right" whale, and so was almost slaughtered to extinction.

STATUS

Endangered. Possibly a population of only 400 worldwide.

Great Right Whale

Wood size: 4" x 4" x 10"

50 to 60 tons

Deep notch in flukes

Thick lips

Note: No neck *see Bowhead*

Horny growths

White patch

Killer Whale

LOCATION

World wide to edge of polar ice fields, common in north Pacific.

SIZE

Male	27 feet to max. 32 feet	8 tons.
Female	23 feet to max. 28 feet	7 tons.
Calf	8 feet.	

COLOR

Velvet black, pale gray saddle behind fin. White from chin to navel. White under flukes, and white eye patch.

FACTS

This extremely intelligent whale is the star at many aquariums. Will eat anything, even other whales; travels in packs.

STATUS

Not endangered.

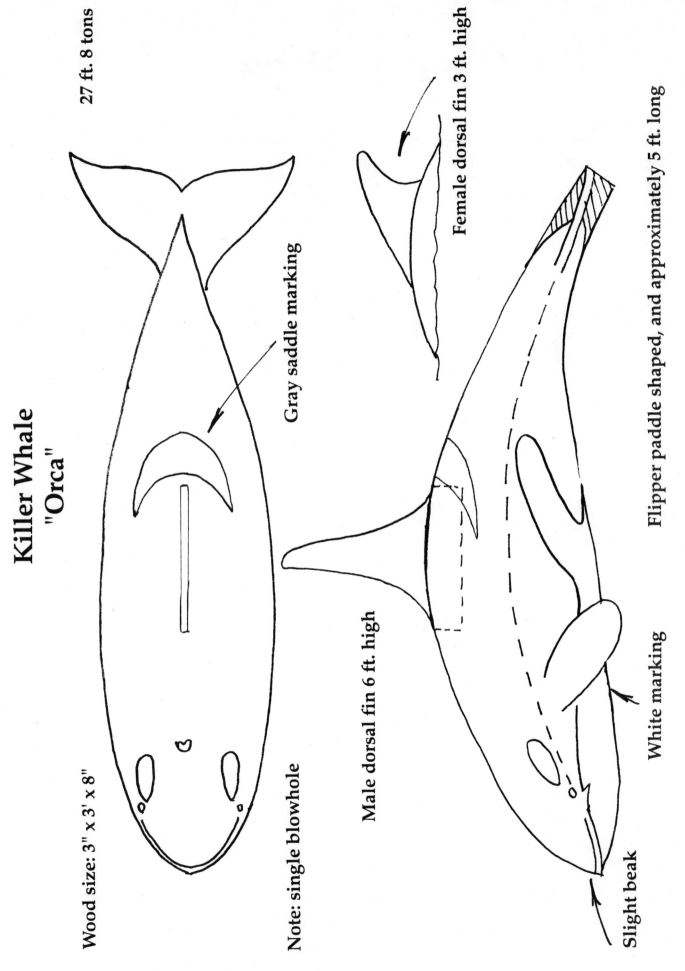

Killer Whale
"Orca"

27 ft. 8 tons

Wood size: 3" x 3' x 8"

Gray saddle marking

Note: single blowhole

Female dorsal fin 3 ft. high

Male dorsal fin 6 ft. high

Flipper paddle shaped, and approximately 5 ft. long

White marking

Slight beak

21

Gray Whale

LOCATION

Northern Pacific to south of the equator.

SIZE

Males	40 feet to max. 50 feet	28 tons
Females	42 feet to max. 50 feet	34 tons
Calf	15 feet	

COLOR

Blue/gray mottled with white and light gray. Baleen gray with yellow edge.

FACTS

This is the most primitive of whales, a bottom feeder that sucks up sediment then filters out the food. This whale arrives in California every winter to mate and bear young.

STATUS

Not endangered in the North Pacific; however, they are no longer found in the Atlantic.

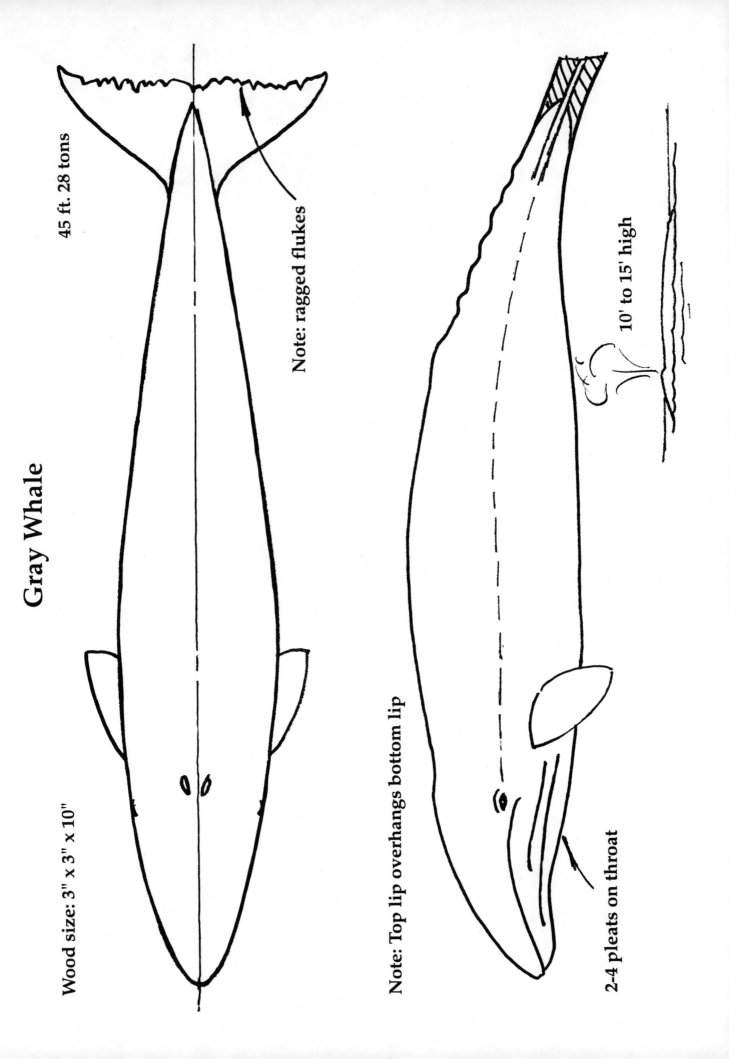

Gray Whale

45 ft. 28 tons

Note: ragged flukes

Wood size: 3" x 3" x 10"

Note: Top lip overhangs bottom lip

2-4 pleats on throat

10' to 15' high

Narwhal
(Unicorn Whale)

LOCATION

Arctic only. Most northerly of all whales.

SIZE

Male	15 feet to max. 20 feet	1.8 tons.
Female	14 feet to max. 17 feet	1 ton.
Calf	5 feet.	

COLOR

White underneath becoming spotted to dark olive brown. Top dark brown; tusk is ivory white.

FACTS

Tusk is spiral, and formed by left tooth growing through lip. Reason for tusk unknown, but Narwhals are now being killed not for their blubber, but for the tusks alone.

STATUS

Believed not endangered.

Narwhal
(Unicorn Whale)

24 ft. 1.8 tons

Wood size: 2" x 3" x 8"

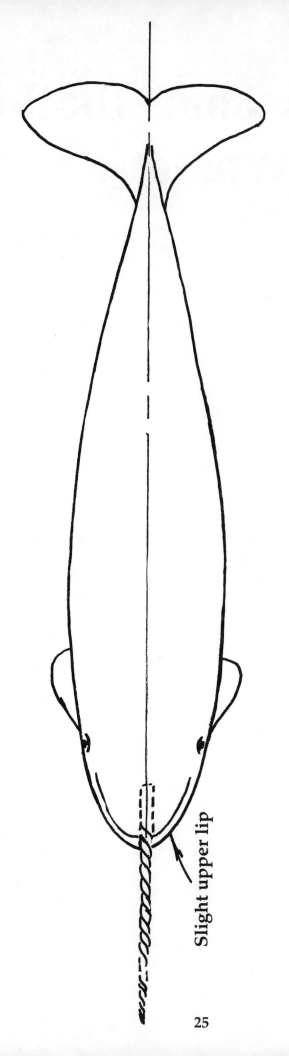

Slight upper lip

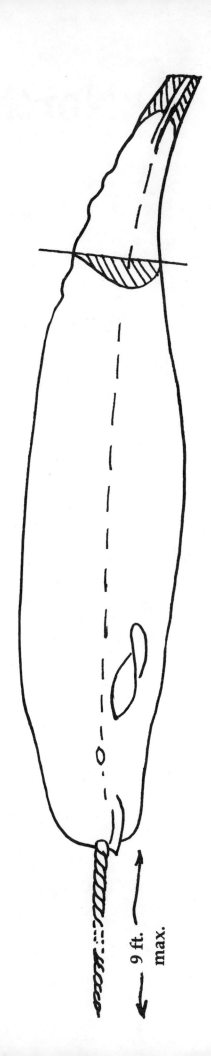

9 ft. max.

25

Northern Four Toothed Whale

LOCATION

North Pacific only.

SIZE

Male	34 feet to max. 40 feet	10 tons.
Female	37 feet to max. 42 feet	10 tons.
Calf	15 feet.	

COLOR

Blue/gray lighter underneath with white patches on navel and between flippers and chin.

FACTS

Largest of beaked whales. They are fast and alert, consequently not too much is known about this species.

STATUS

Not endangered.

Northern Four Toothed Whale

Wood size: 3" x 4" x 10"

34 ft. 40 tons

Note: No notch in flukes

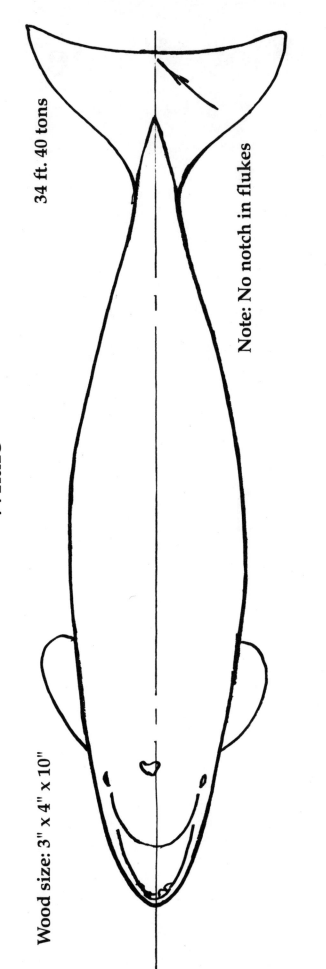

Note: Small dorsal fin

4 pleats in throat

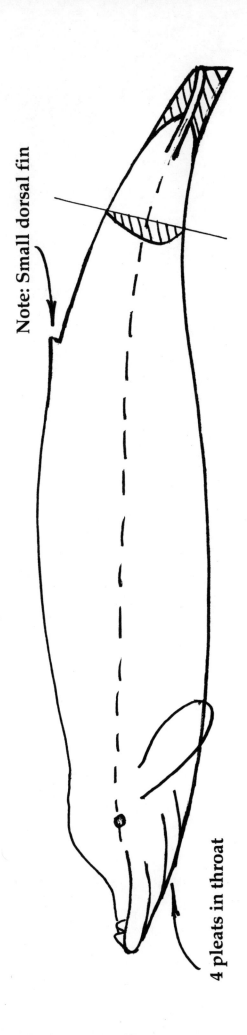

Longfin Pilot Whale

LOCATION

North Atlantic, southern Indian Ocean, South Pacific, South Atlantic, not in equatorial regions.

SIZE

Male	20 feet to max. 28 feet	4 tons.
Female	16 feet to max. 20 feet	2 tons
Calf	6 feet.	

COLOR

Black, dark gray saddle behind dorsal fin, white patch from throat to navel.

FACTS

Stranding is very common with this species. In Faroe Islands they are stampeded by inhabitants forcing them ashore, and 1,500 are killed each summer.

STATUS

Possibly endangered.

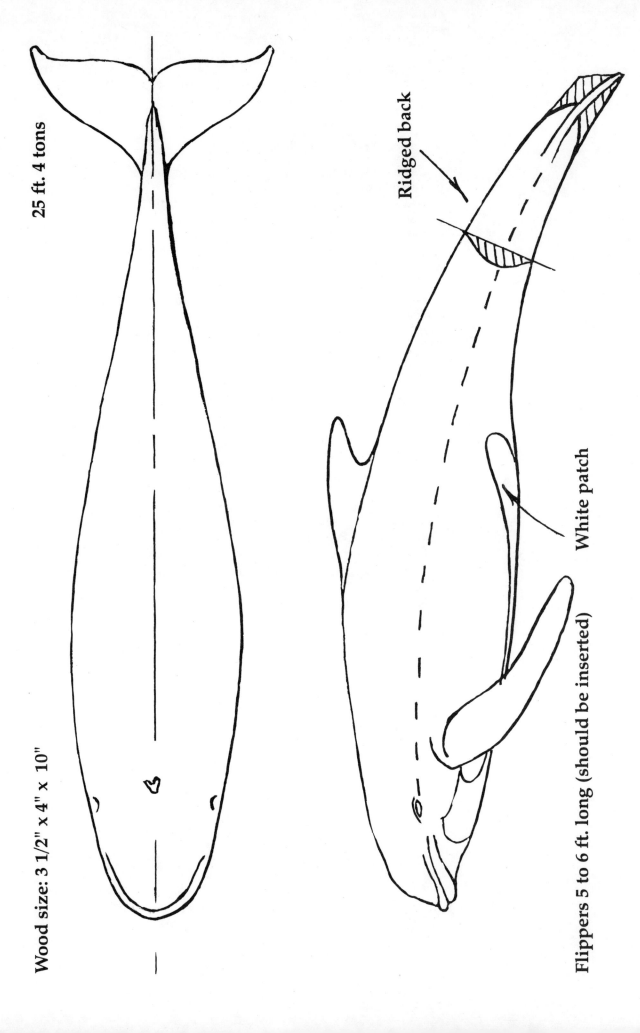

Longfin Pilot Whale

25 ft. 4 tons

Wood size: 3 1/2" x 4" x 10"

Ridged back

White patch

Flippers 5 to 6 ft. long (should be inserted)

Carving Tips

Use a good sharp knife. Accidents occur when you push hard on a dull blade and slip.

Always pencil in where you want your knife to go—no guesswork.

Remember you can't put it back once you've carved it off. So don't rush. Sit back, put your feet up, and carve away.

I hope you will enjoy carving some, or all, of the whales in this book. I know that when I first carved them I was impressed and awed by their size and gentleness.

During the research involved in this project, I also became aware of the sad plight of all sea mammals. Man's motives are really difficult to understand.

In the last century, and the early part of this century, there was a need for baleen, blubber and oil. These "products" were needed by a developing society. Surely now with the advantages of modern technology all of these "products" could be manufactured. Yet at this time two nations; Japan and Norway are continuing to hunt these mysterious creatures—FOR WHAT ?!!.

Listed below are some of the books I used as reference material. I fully recommend all of them as interesting reading.They will also help you as you carve and paint your whale.

BONNER, NIGEL. 1989. *Whales of the World.*
ELLIS, RICHARD. 1991. *Men and Whales.* (great history)
HOYT, ERICH. 1988 *The Whales of Canada.*
WATSON, LYALL. 1981. *Sea Guide to Whales of the World.* (excellent)

Painting Tips

I use acrylic paints. They dry fast, are durable and water soluble. They can be readily obtained at art stores, hobby shops and craft centers.

It's better to paint the carving in two or three stages and build up the color, than to try to cover it in one coat.

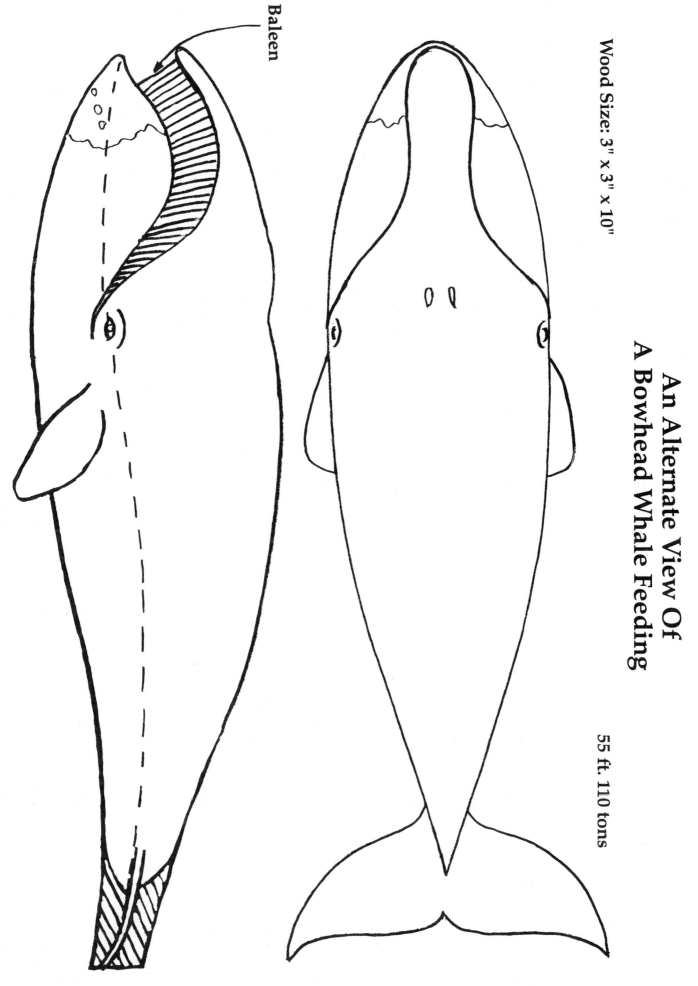

Baleen

Wood Size: 3" x 3" x 10"

An Alternate View Of
A Bowhead Whale Feeding

55 ft. 110 tons

Carving the
Great Right Whale

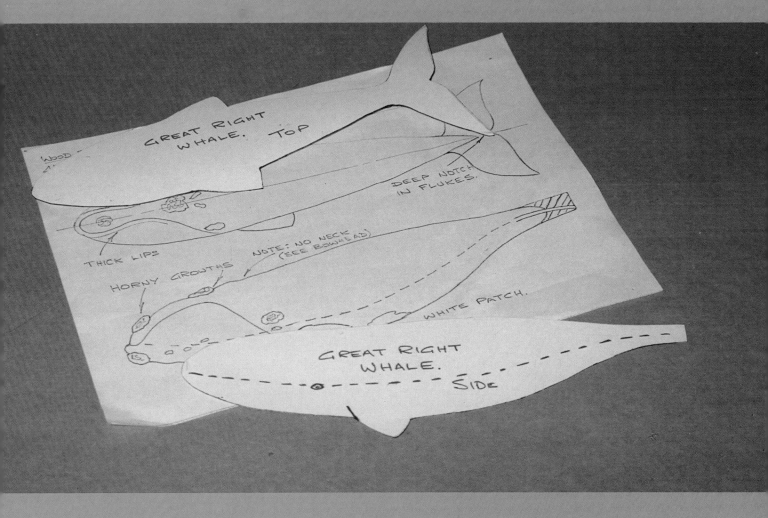

Trace the drawings onto heavy cardboard, cut them out and save them for future carvings.

Place templates on top and side of wooden block and draw around them.

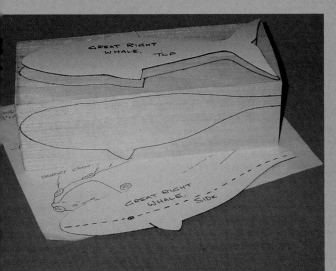

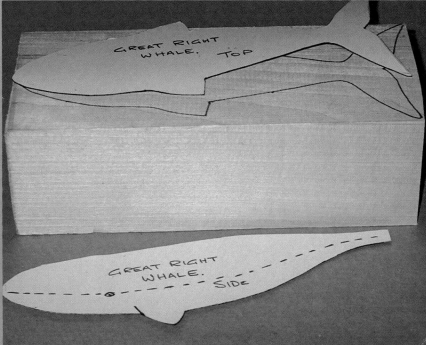

Now saw the whale out, top view first. Do not saw the line all the way through, leave 1/16", this will snap off later.

Now saw the side view.

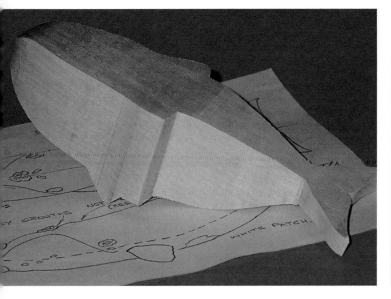

Split the block apart leaving the rough-sawn whale.

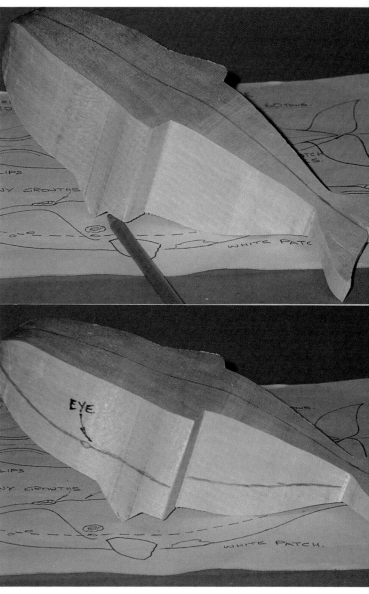

Draw center lines down the back and the belly, then on the sides. The lines on the sides pass through the eyes (this is usually the widest part of the whale's body), and end at the center of the flukes.

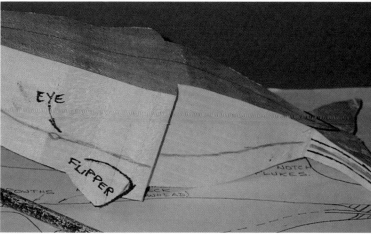

Draw on the flippers.

34

Draw the direction of the flukes.

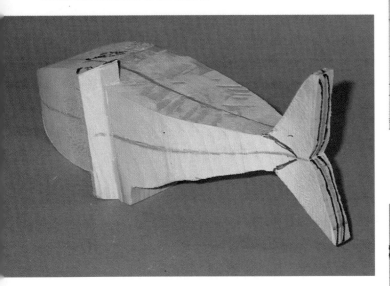

Carve out the flippers roughly, do not take off too much wood at this time.

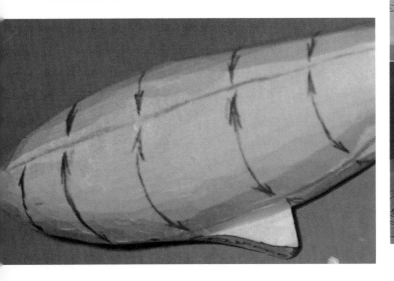

Now round the whale carving from line to line. Do not carve the line out, this will change the shape of the whale.

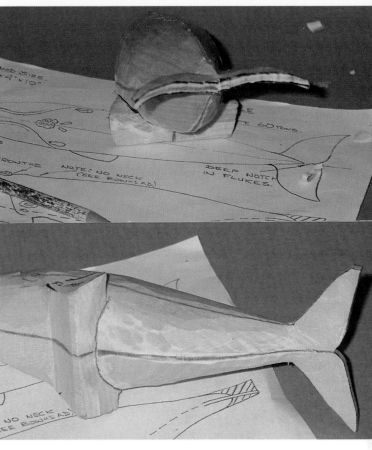

Carefully carve the flukes. Do not carve them too thin at this time as they are fairly fragile.

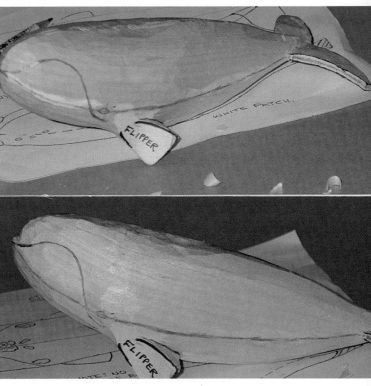

Draw, and then carve the mouth. Use the location of the eyes to help you obtain symmetry, note that the corner of the mouth is underneath the eye.

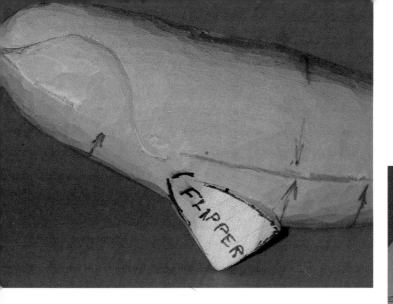

Draw the eyes to the correct shape and carve them. The size is 1/8". should you wish to use glass eyes, simply drill a 1/8" hole and insert them. I have used both methods.

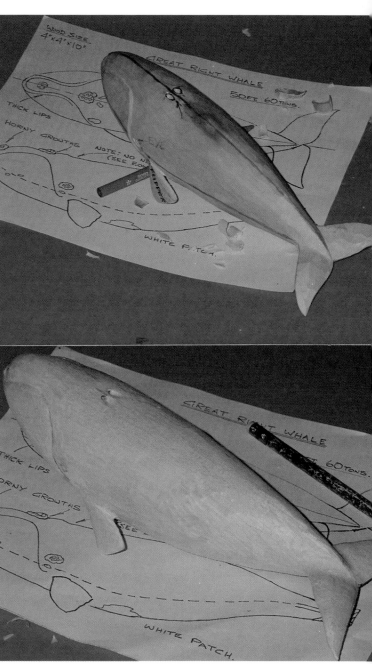

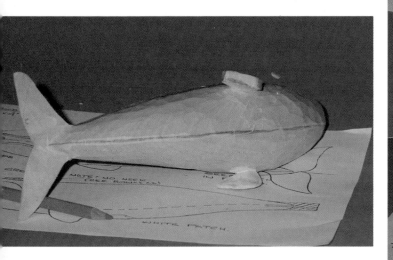

Now finish carving under the flippers, be gentle, leave them about 1/8" thick.

Carve the blowholes. Two small indentations will do. It's not necessary to drill holes.

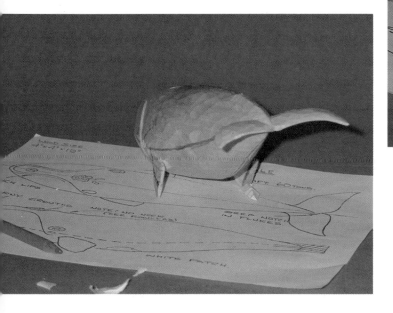

Finish carving the flukes. Here once again go gently.

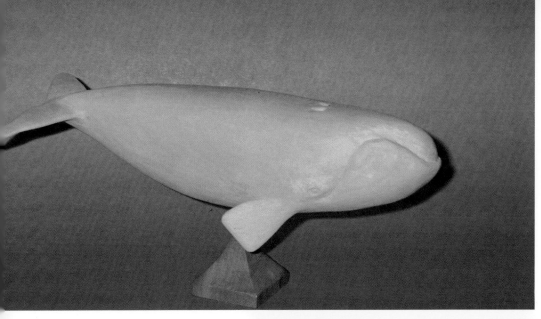

Completely sand the carving all over. Make sure all edges are soft.

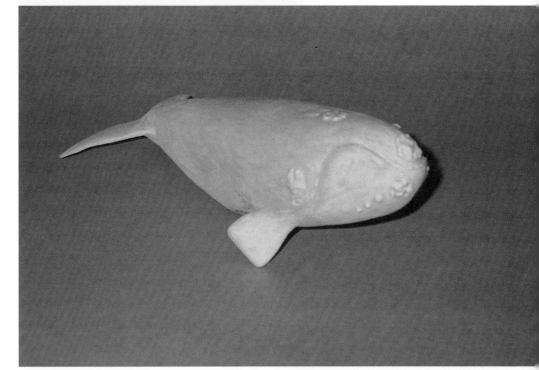

For the "horny growths" on the chin, nose, eyes, etc., I use a water soluble wood dough, and stipple it on.

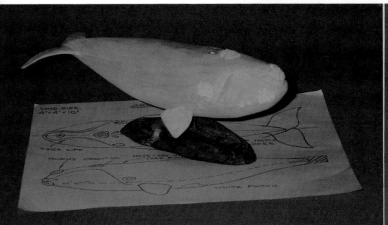

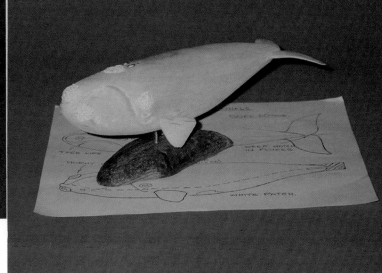

We are all finished carving. If you wish to stain or varnish your whale go ahead. If you want to paint it, we'll go into that later.

Carving a Killer Whale

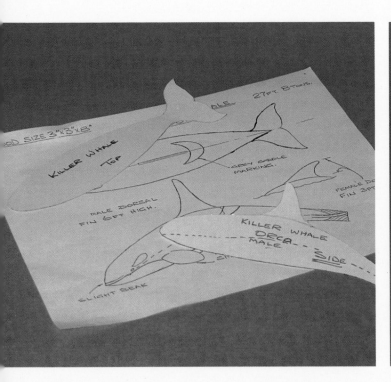

Trace drawing onto a piece of heavy cardboard. Do not trace flippers or flukes. These will be inserted in this carving.

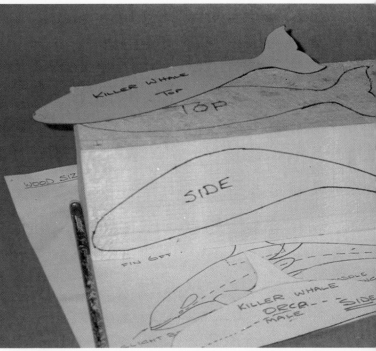

Place templates on top of block and draw top view.

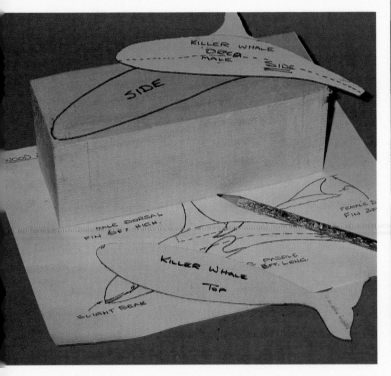

Place templates on block. Draw side view.

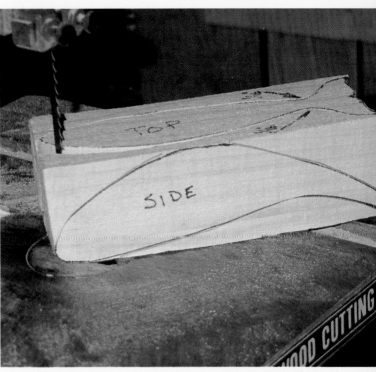

Saw out, but do not saw the line completely through. Leave 1/16" allowing you to carve through the side pattern. When both views are cut, snap off the excess.

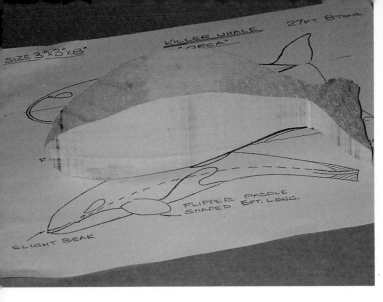

Split wood apart.

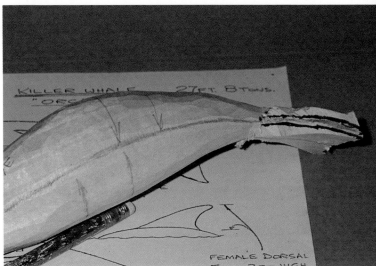

Round the body from line to line, do not carve the line out.

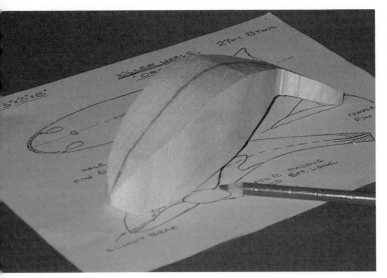

Draw center line on top and belly.

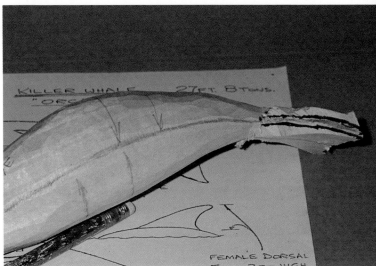

Draw lines on the flukes to indicate which way you want them to flow.

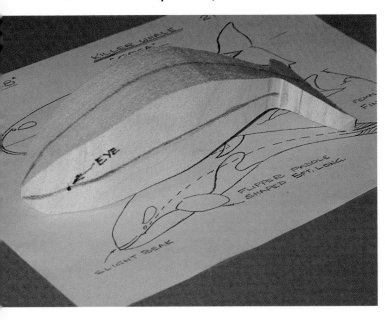

Draw side line. Make sure this passes through the eyes.

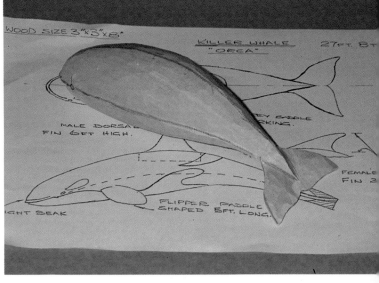

Now rough carve the flukes, very carefully--not too thin.

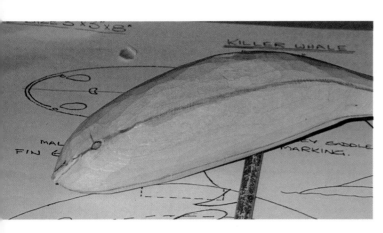

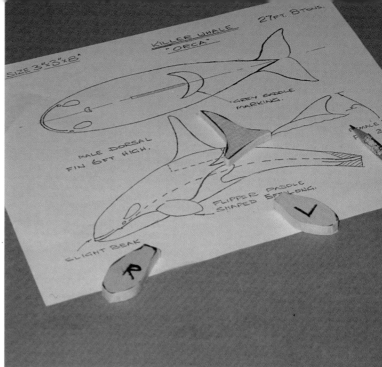

Draw and carve the mouth. Use the eyes to locate the corners of the mouth; watch for symmetry.

Trace the flippers and fin onto a piece of 1/4" wood and saw them out. Make sure there are left and right flippers.

Lay out and carve the slots for the flippers (1/4" x 3/8"), and the dorsal fin (1/4" x 1 1/2").

Glue the dorsal and pectoral fins in place. Now carve them so that they blend into the body.

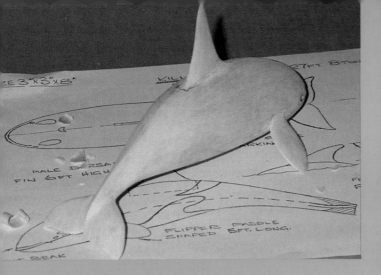

Finish carving the flukes. Make them a little less than an 1/8" thick. Do the same with the flippers.

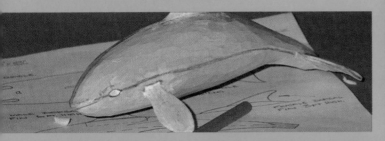

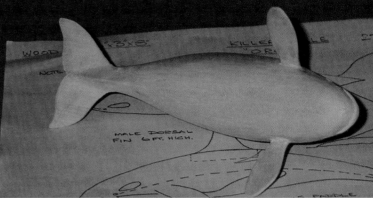

Now softly sand the whale carving smooth all over, with no hard lines anywhere. Remember these sleek creatures are designed for underwater travel.

Carve the eyes. They are approximately 1/8" in diameter. You can drill a 1/8" hole and insert glass eyes if you wish. I have used both methods.

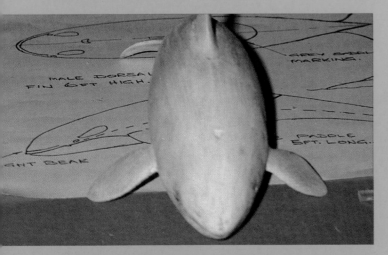

Carve the blowhole. A single small indentation will do.

Here are two views of the finished carving, I hope yours has turned out well.

Painting a Great Right Whale

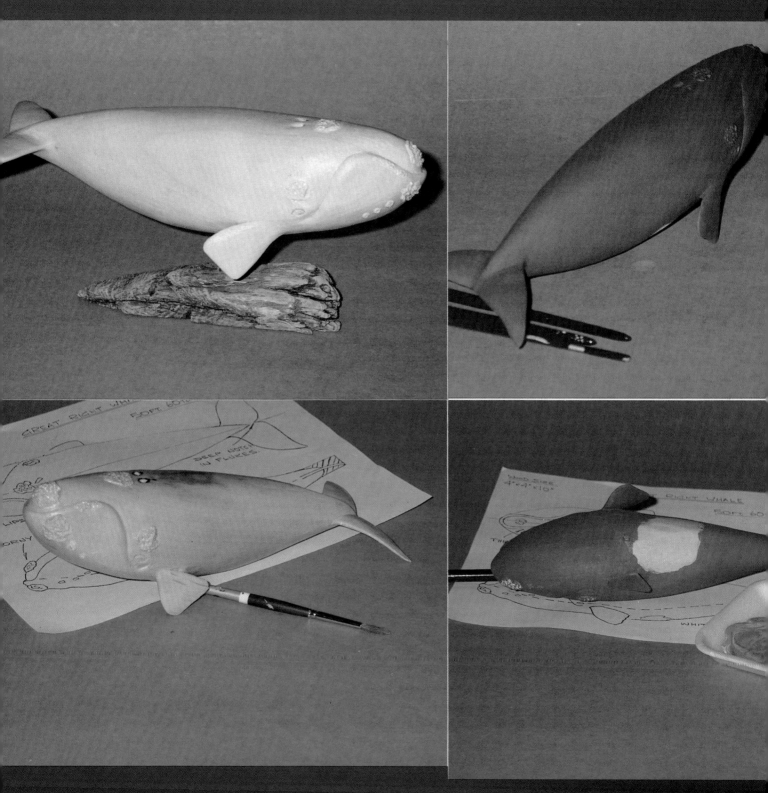

Seal the wood. Use urethane, shellac, or any of the many sealers available on the market. Then lightly sand using 200 grit sand paper.

Paint the whole whale light grey, except for the white belly patch.

Now paint the white belly patch.

Paint the body a blueish-black.

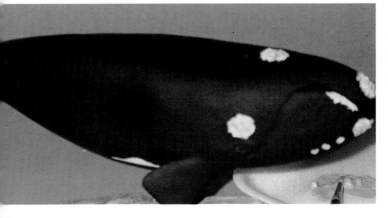

Paint the "growths" on the chin and head white, with a slight yellow tinge.

The eyes should be painted, light gray, with a black pupil.

A coat of varnish will protect the paint.

The completed Great Right Whale.

Painting a Killer Whale

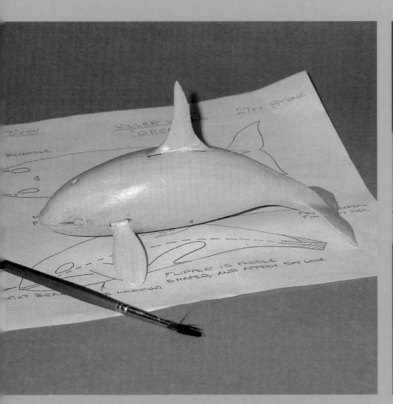

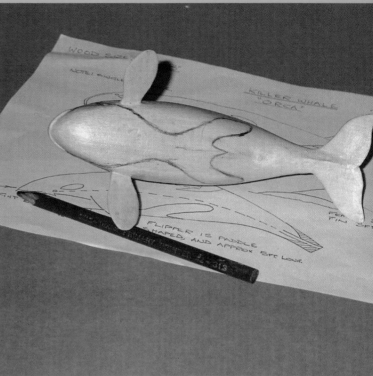

Seal the wood. Use urethane, shellac etc., then lightly sand the whale using 200 grit sandpaper.

Sketch in the line between the black and white areas. Note that from below it resembles an "arrow."

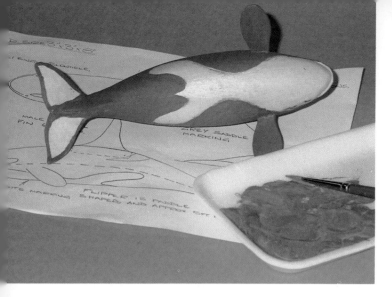

Paint the whale light gray.

Paint the belly and chin white. Continue with the white paint on the undersides of the flukes. Always make sure your painting is symmetrical.

Now paint the rest of the whale black with a little deep blue mixed in with it.

Now a coat of varnish to protect the paint.

Paint the eyes pale gray with black pupils, and also paint the white eye patches.

Paint the gray saddle, behind the dorsal fin.

Here are two views of the completed carving.

46

Three Killer whales.

Gray whale. (carved eyes).

Humpback whale. (carved eyes).

Long fin pilot whale. (inserted glass eyes).

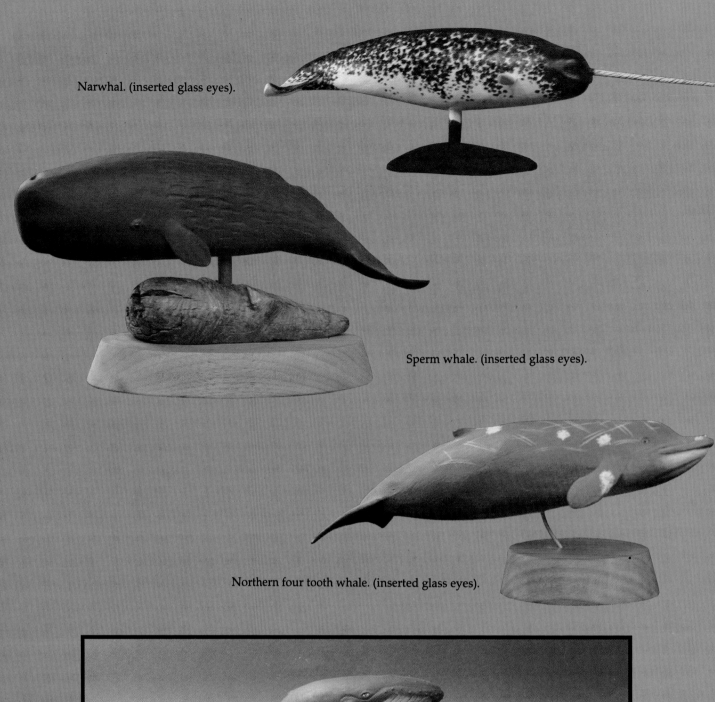

Narwhal. (inserted glass eyes).

Sperm whale. (inserted glass eyes).

Northern four tooth whale. (inserted glass eyes).